THE GOOD APPLE HOMEWORK HELPER

by Jeri S. Cipriano

Good Apple

For Rachel, who has always insisted on
doing everything herself!

Editor: Suzanne Moyers

© Good Apple
A Division of Frank Schaffer Publications, Inc.
23740 Hawthorne Boulevard
Torrance, CA 90505-5927

2 3 4 5 6 7 8 9   MAL 01 00 99 98

TO THE STUDENT

In this book, you'll find time-saving tips on everything you need to know about homework, getting organized, and doing well in school. Many of the tips come from real experts—kids like you who have found great ways to get things done.

You probably won't want to read this book cover to cover. Instead, take a few moments to review the Table of Contents and see what's inside. Flip through the pages to get a better idea of the topics. Read a few of the sections you're most interested in. Look at the handy "Clip and Save" section at the end of each section and cut out a few of these pages to put in your school notebook.

TO THE TEACHER OR PARENT

This book provides students with simple, practical advice to help them do their work more independently, with greater success. If you're a teacher, you may want to reproduce and distribute all or part of a section at one time or supplement sections with tips of your own. Parents will want to share this book with children, encouraging them to work independently, but reminding them that they should ask for help when they need it.

CONTENTS

PART 1

DEVELOPING GOOD HABITS

It's true: Homework can be hard. But it doesn't have to be. A big part of doing homework well is being organized and managing your time. In this section, you'll

- test your homework habits;
- pick up time-saving tips from other kids;
- set goals;
- design personal schedules;

and much more.

HOMEWORK HABITS INVENTORY

Oh, no! A pop quiz — already!

Don't worry. There are no right or wrong answers on this test. But all answers count because each one tells you something important about yourself. Put a check in the column that best describes you.

	Yes	No	Well, sort of
I have a homework assignment book.			
I write down all assignments.			
I keep track of due dates for all work.			
I have a big calendar at home to highlight important dates.			
I keep a dictionary handy when I do my homework.			
I have a copy of my school schedule in my notebook.			
I have a copy of my school schedule at home.			
When I write down my homework, I include the book I need to bring home.			
I check my bookbag before I leave for school and before I come home.			
I have the phone number of a classmate in case I have a question about homework.			
I have a regular time and place for homework each day.			

It's pretty easy to figure out how this quiz works.
The more *yes* answers you have, the better organized you are.

Look over your answers. Choose two *no* answers you think you could change to *yes*. Write what (and how) you'll change, below.

_____

_____

_____

SET UP YOUR WORKSPACE

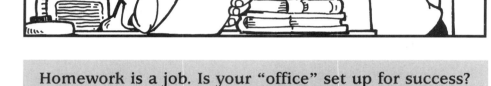

Homework is a job. Is your "office" set up for success?
Check all the sentences that are true.

- ❑ I have pens and pencils.
- ❑ I have paper.
- ❑ I have a dictionary.
- ❑ I have a ruler.
- ❑ I have enough quiet in which to work.
- ❑ I have enough space to spread out.
- ❑ I have a watch or clock to help me keep track of time.
- ❑ I have adequate lighting in my homework area.
- ❑ I have a comfortable chair.
- ❑ I have privacy when I need it.
- ❑ I keep extra supplies for special projects (graph paper, construction paper, tape, scissors).

Write down one thing you'd like to change about your homework space. What can you do to make it better? Write your idea below.

_____

_____

_____

GET ASSIGNMENTS STRAIGHT

Read the assignment pads on this page to see how two students might write down the homework their teacher has assigned. Which student would you call if you were absent from school?

"Read pages 10–12 in your math book and do the "challenge" section at the bottom of page 12. On page 12 of your math workbook, do examples 1–5 and 10–15. Read chapter 3 in *The Sign of the Beaver* and, in your journals, predict what will happen next. Write neatly in ink. Study the 10 new spelling words. There'll be a spelling test on Friday."

Math book: pp.10–12,
Challenge (p.12)
Workbook: p.12: 1–5, 10–15.
Beaver: chapter 3.
Journal: What happens next?
Neat. In ink.
Spelling Test Friday!!

Susie

Math: pp.10–12:
Challenge, 1–5 and 10–15
Read chapter 3.
Make predictions.
Test Friday.

Kirk

Which student left out key facts? _____

What problems could result?

_____

_____

Whenever you get an assignment, ask yourself:

- What *exactly* do I have to do?
- When is it due?
- What do I need to take home?
- Are there any special instructions I need to follow?

TAKE A TIP FROM A KID: ABOUT ASSIGNMENTS

Use a highlighter to set apart important information in your homework pad.

Read the directions twice before you start anything. Use your own words to explain to yourself, out loud, what you need to do.

Use shorthand and scrap paper to do the "thinking" part of your work, then you won't have so much to recopy on your final draft. You'll also save good paper.

Keep all school supplies in one place, like in a box or drawer.

Do as much homework as you can in school. That way you can ask your teacher for help if you need it.

Make friends with someone who's good in a subject you're not. Become homework buddies.

Reread everything! Check for what you may have left out.

Save all homework. It's a fast way to review for a test.

Check the tips you already use.

Star the ones you're willing to try.

Add any good tips you and your classmates think up.

My Own Homework Tips _____

_____

Tips From My Classmates _____

_____

See *Clip and Save: Day by Day*, page 24

SETTING PRIORITIES

Sometimes, there isn't enough time to do everything you want to do in one day. That's why it's important to learn how to plan your time, so you can do the most important things first. That's called setting priorities.

Pretend you have the following list of things you need to do. Arrange the events in order of priority by putting a 1 next to the most important event, a 2 next to the second most important event, and so on.

- ☐ RSVP to party invitation.
- ☐ Practice piano.
- ☐ Work on book report due in three days.
- ☐ Study for tomorrow's spelling test.
- ☐ Start Colonial Times diorama.
- ☐ Count money in savings account.
- ☐ Get parent's signature for school trip at end of week.
- ☐ Write thank-you note to aunt for last week's present.
- ☐ Call friends to find out weekend plans.

Suppose you don't have time to do everything on the list. Star the items you could save for another day.

Now think of three things you absolutely want to do today. Write them in order of importance on the line below.

_____

_____

_____

TIME OUT!

Do you have enough time for everything you need to do? A schedule can help you get as many things done as possible. Before you make a schedule, though, it's a good idea to find out exactly how you already spend your time.

Look at the Week-at-a-Glance chart below. The numbers under each day stand for how many hours one kid spent doing each thing. Fill in your own chart on the next page. Remember: Your total hours each day should add up to about 24 hours.

	Mon.	Tues.	Wed.	Thurs.	Fri.	Sat.	Sun.
Sleeping	10	9	10	$9\frac{1}{2}$	10	10	10
Eating	1	1	$1\frac{1}{2}$	1	$1\frac{1}{2}$	$1\frac{1}{2}$	2
Dressing, showering, exercising	1	1	$1\frac{1}{2}$	1	$1\frac{1}{2}$	$1\frac{1}{2}$	$1\frac{1}{2}$
School	7	7	7	7	7	0	0
Homework	$\frac{1}{2}$	1	$\frac{3}{4}$	$\frac{3}{4}$	0	0	$\frac{1}{2}$
Sports & Clubs	$1\frac{1}{2}$	0	2	1	3	2	0
Lessons/Practice	$\frac{1}{2}$	1	$\frac{1}{2}$	$\frac{1}{2}$	0	$\frac{1}{2}$	0
Chores	$\frac{1}{4}$	$\frac{1}{4}$	$\frac{1}{2}$	$\frac{1}{4}$	$\frac{1}{4}$	1	0
Shopping	1/2	0	0	2	0	1	0
Entertainment (TV/Computer/Games)	1	1	$\frac{1}{2}$	1	3	2	2
Time with Friends (in person; on phone)	0	$\frac{1}{2}$	0	1	1	2	2
Time with Family	$\frac{1}{2}$	1	0	1	0	2	3
Bedtime/Time Alone (reading, writing, hobbies)	$\frac{1}{2}$	$\frac{3}{4}$	$\frac{1}{2}$	2	$\frac{1}{2}$	$\frac{1}{2}$	2
Other things	0	0	0	2	0	0	1
HOURS	$24\frac{1}{4}$	$23\frac{1}{2}$	$24\frac{3}{4}$	30	$27\frac{3}{4}$	24	24

TiME TRACKING

For the Week of _____

	Mon.	Tues.	Wed.	Thurs.	Fri.	Sat.	Sun.
Sleeping **Eating**							
Dressing, showering, exercising							
School **Homework** **Sports & Clubs**							
Lessons/Practice							
Chores							
Shopping							
Entertainment (TV/Computer/Games)							
Time with Friends (in person; on phone)							
Time with Family							
Bedtime/Time Alone (reading, writing, hobbies)							
Other things							
HOURS							

TAKE A TIP FROM A KID: FIRST THINGS FIRST

Do your homework right away. Then you'll have the rest of the night free.

Do hard assignments first or whenever you have the most energy.

Don't wait until the last minute to do assignments. If a crisis comes up, you may not finish in time. Work on long-range projects a little at a time.

Assign a set time and place each day for homework. For instance, at 4:00 P.M., go to your room, sit at your desk, and start working. Pretty soon it will become a habit.

Tell your teacher if you're having trouble with your homework. Teachers are there to help.

Ask an older sister or brother for help when you need it. You can do them a favor in return.

Ask your teacher if you can use self-stick labels you've prepared ahead to save time writing your name on every paper.

Check the tips you already use.

Star the ones you're willing to try.

Add any good tips you and your classmates thought up.

My Timesaving Tips _____

_____

My Classmates' Timesaving Tips_____

_____

WEEK AT A GLANCE

Here's one kid's schedule for the week ahead. Use it to help you fill in your own schedule on the next page.

	MON.	TUES.	WED.	THURS.	FRI.	SAT.	SUN.
6 AM to 8 AM	Wake, dress and leave for school. →					*(Feed Guinea Pig)*	*(Feed Guinea Pig)*
8 AM to 12 PM	School	🎵	School	🎵		Swim team	Religion
12 PM to 3 PM					🎵		
3 PM to 5 PM	*(Walk dog)*	Homework / Homework	Religion	*(Walk dog)*	Homework	*(Walk dog)*	*(Walk dog)*
5 PM to 7 PM	Dinner	Dinner	Dinner			Dinner	Dinner
7 PM to 9 PM		Swim team			Swim team		
___ AM to ___ PM	← Read → Sleep						

KEY

 Chorus

 Piano

 Sleep

 Walk dog

Swim team

School

Dinner

 Read

 Feed Guinea Pig

Homework

Religion

Wake, dress and leave for school

MY WEEK AT A GLANCE

- Copy this page before you fill it out in case you need to make any changes later.

- Use colored markers for the various activities. Use the same colors to fill in the key.

- Look at each day. Ask yourself
  Do I have enough time for homework?
  Do I have enough time for relaxing?
  Are there any changes I can make in my schedule?

If you decide to make changes, use your extra copy of this page to redo the schedule.

	MON.	TUES.	WED.	THURS.	FRI.	SAT.	SUN.
6 AM to 8 AM							
8 AM to 12 PM							
12 PM to 3 PM							
3 PM to 5 PM							
5 PM to 7 PM							
7 PM to 9 PM							
___ AM to ___ PM							

KEY ☐ ☐

☐ ☐

☐ ☐ ☐

☐ ☐ ☐

TV Time

If you're like most kids, you probably watch TV.

The chart on the next page will help you organize your TV watching so that you have time left over to enjoy other kinds of fun. Follow these steps to fill out the chart:

- Look at the TV listings and choose some shows you'd like to watch.
- Write in your reasons for watching (to be with the family, to learn something, just for fun).
- At the end of each day, write down the names of the shows you actually watched. Jot down what you thought about each show.
- At the end of the week, look over the chart. Did you watch more or less TV than you had planned? Did you really learn something or enjoy what you watched? Do you think you used your TV time wisely?

Take a Tip From a Kid

Here are some ideas for avoiding all those fights about who watches which shows. It'll also help you plan your TV-watching time so you can do other things.

When you get Sunday's paper, look over the TV listings for the week with the whole family. Let everyone initial one or two programs they really want to watch.

Hang up the daily listings so everyone can see who will be watching what, when!

Work out a system for deciding what to do when two people want to watch different shows at the same time. (Especially if you have just one TV set.)

With your family, plan a no-TV night. Play boardgames, listen to music, or do whatever you enjoy—together.

TV TIME WORKSHEET

DAY	I PLAN TO WATCH (Programs)	Reasons	I WATCHED (Programs)	Reasons	Opinion
Monday					
Tuesday					
Wednesday					
Thursday					
Friday					
Saturday					
Sunday					

BREAKING HABITS, MAKING HABITS

Do you want to break some bad habits and pick up some good ones? Here's how.

Write Down Your Goals

What bad habit would you like to quit? By when? What good habit would you like to start? By when? Write down your goals. Put them where you can see them often—on the closet door, the ceiling, or the bathroom mirror.

Make Yourself a Star

Each week, write your goal for the week in the Sunday square on a wall calendar. Paste or draw a star on each day that you accomplish what you've set out to do. Promise yourself a special treat for every 10, 15, or 25 stars you earn.

Take Small Steps

Pick one goal to work on. Do your best to reach that goal for one week. Then try a new goal the next week.

Don't Expect Perfection

You're determined to stop biting your nails. But then one day, there you are, chewing your fingers again. Instead of thinking: "I'll never stop!" remind yourself how hard it is to break habits. Don't give up; keep focused on your goal.

Believe in Yourself

Stay positive. Don't say, "I think I can do this." Instead, tell yourself, "I know I can do this. I will do this."

Picture the New You

Three times a day, picture yourself as you'd like to be.

Suppose you are trying to give up junk food. Imagine yourself eating a juicy apple or a banana. Picture yourself looking healthy and fit. Imagine how good you'll feel.

Hook Up with a Buddy

Team up with someone who also wants to break a habit or set a new goal, even if it's different from yours. Celebrate each others' successes.

Be a Copy Cat!

Think of someone you admire. Figure out what you like about that person. Try behaving in a similar way. From time to time, stop and ask yourself, "What would so-and-so do now?" or "Is this the way so-and-so would handle this situation?"

Make a Habit of Success

When you accomplish something difficult, it often sets the stage for other successes. Use your new confidence to try making more changes.

Write down some old habits you'd like to break:

_____

_____

Write down some new habits you'd like to develop:

_____

_____

PUT IT IN WRITING

A contract is an agreement or promise you make with someone else to reach a certain goal. Use this form to make a contract with yourself to reach some important goals. Add your signature at the bottom. (If you want to be especially official, ask someone to sign as a "witness" to the promise you've made.)

My Contract

This year, **a habit I will break is** _____
_____
_____

I will try to reach my goal by (date) _____

To reach my goal, I will do the following: _____
_____
_____

For starters, this week I will _____
_____
_____

This year, **a habit I will develop is** _____
_____
_____

I will try to reach my goal by (date) _____

To make my goal, I will do the following: _____
_____

For starters, this week I will _____

Date: _____

Signature: _____

Witness: _____

SEAL OF APPROVAL

SELF-IMPROVEMENT PLEDGE

A pledge is a promise you make to yourself or someone else.

Make a pledge to try something challenging. Here are some examples of things you could pledge to do:

- Read a book for one hour each day;
- Practice piano for one-half hour a day;
- Tutor a younger sister or brother;
- Work on a special hobby every day.

Schedule the amount of time you are willing to spend working on your goal each day. Then record the actual time you spent and what you accomplished. When you're done, give yourself a pat on the back!

My Pledge to Myself

This week, I pledge to _____

_____

for a certain amount of time each day.

Scheduled Time	Actual Time	What I Accomplished (pages read, songs rehearsed, and so on)
Sun.		
Mon.		
Tues.		
Wed.		
Thurs.		
Fri.		
Sat.		

Go For The Goal

Congratulations! You're on a roll!

Now write four weekly goals for the **month.** Mark each day you worked toward achieving your goal. At the end of each week, give yourself a reward.

Goals I Want to Reach

1. _____

2. _____

3. _____

4. _____

Mon.	Tues.	Wed.	Thurs.	Fri.	Sat.	Sun.	Reward

Why interrupt a winning streak? To see even more improvement, continue pursuing your goals for another two months.

Mon.	Tues.	Wed.	Thurs.	Fri.	Sat.	Sun.	Reward

Mon.	Tues.	Wed.	Thurs.	Fri.	Sat.	Sun.	Reward

Clip and Save

DAY BY DAY

Create your own handy homework pad using this page as a guide.

- Use a hole-punch to add these pages to your looseleaf notebook.
- Each day, write the date at the top of the page.
- Write your homework assignments according to subject. Note when each assignment is due, and put a check when you've completed it.
- Use the bottom of the page to jot down important information.

Today is _____

Day of Week   Month   Date   Year

SUBJECT	HOMEWORK	DUE
Reading	☐ completed	_____
Math	☐ completed	_____
Social Studies	☐ completed	_____
Language Arts	☐ completed	_____
Spelling	☐ completed	_____
Science	☐ completed	_____
Music/Art	☐ completed	_____
Computer/Library	☐ completed	_____

Things to Remember

After School: _____

Take Home: _____

Bring to School: _____

MONTH BY MONTH

Congratulations! By now you should be officially organized.

Make copies of this monthly calendar page and keep it with you the whole year. Fill in important events or reminders in the correct dates.

Calendar for the Month of _____

Saturday				
Friday				
Thursday				
Wednesday				
Tuesday				
Monday				
Sunday				

PART 2

GETTING DOWN TO BUSINESS

Now that you know *when* to do your homework, it's time to learn *how*. No, we're not going to do all those long division problems for you. That's your job! But we will give you some great ideas for helping you do your work better in less time.

In this chapter, you'll learn how to sharpen your memory, take notes like a pro, and pick up shortcuts for doing math, social studies, and science homework, among other things.

Mind Over Matter

1776. 3 × 4 = 12. Tuba lessons are on Tuesday...
You've got a lot to remember!

Here's an idea that will help: Your memory likes unusual information or facts that stand out in some way. Think about how using different color notebooks for each subject makes it a lot easier to find the right one in that crowded locker when you're in a hurry. Pairing facts with interesting cues works the same way.

Write it down.
Keep a pad and pencil with you at all times. Look back at your notes often to refresh your memory.

Talk to yourself.
Say things out loud at least three times. This technique is especially good for remembering a shopping list, a spelling list, or any other list of facts.

Try saying things in different ways, too: in a deep voice, a squeaky voice, loudly, softly, and as a song. Find the rhythm in a group of related ideas.

Picture it.

Suppose you want to remember that the word *surprise* is spelled with an s at the end, not a z. Just picture a silly snake hiding in the word. It also helps to remember the way groups of facts are presented on a notebook or textbook page.

Make up a silly sentence.

My **V**ery **E**ducated **M**other **J**ust **S**erved **U**s **N**ine **P**ickles. Almost everyone has used this saying to remember the order of the nine planets. The first letter of each word in the sentence stands for one of the planets.

Ask yourself questions.

Think about what you have to do. When you leave for school, ask yourself: Do I have what I need? My homework? My keys? What am I doing after school?

Do something weird.

Tie a yellow ribbon on your finger and think: This will remind me to take the bus home today instead of the carpool. Or switch your watch to your other wrist to remember that you need to walk the neighbor's dog. These strange cues will jolt your memory.

Put things in order.

Do you sometimes need to remember events in order, like certain events leading up to an important event in history? Just picture the events happening from left to right in your room — on your curtains, your bureau, your floor. When you need to remember the events, just think of the things in your room — in order.

Review information when it's fresh.

Did you know that people forget almost half of what they learn within 30 minutes? To make new material stick in your mind, look at each day's notes when you get home from school. Then go over them again every few days. Don't wait until test time to review.

REMEMBER THIS!

Suppose you have to remember the things below. Help your memory by making up a silly picture for each example. See if a friend can guess what each picture means.

1. Your dad sends you to the store to buy bread, dog food, milk, and donuts.

2. You have a karate lesson on Wednesday. On Thursday, you have to go to the eye doctor.

3. You have to go to the library for the following books: a book about rockets, a book about monkeys, a book about Walt Disney, and a book about pirates.

4. You're meeting your friend at the mall at 4:15 in front of the pet shop. Then you're going shopping for boots, jeans, and a notebook.

THANKS FOR THE MEMORIES

Flex your mental muscles with memory games, or mnemonics (say: *nih-MAH-niks;* the first *m* is silent). Mnemonics is just a fancy way of describing how you connect what you need to remember with what you already know. Here's how mnemonics can work for you in school.

Spell Check

Are there certain words you can't seem to remember how to spell? Make up mental connections that will help you.

Connect the meaning of the word with its spelling.

> De**ss**ert or desert?
> Dessert has **"two helpings"** of *s*'s; desert has only one *s*.

> Principle or principal?
> A princi**pal** is your **pal**

> Stationery or stationary?
> Station**er**y is pap**er**

Focus on the problem area of the word.

> A ba**ll**oon is a hollow ba**ll**.
> Expen**$**es have to do with **$**.
> Knowl**edge** gives one an **edge** in life.
> If it is perman**ent**, it won't **dent**.
> M**ne**monics is looking at **m**emory in a **ne**w way.

Do the double letters in the word committee give you trouble?
You could think: **Committee . . . three doubles . . . mm, tt, ee**.

Facts on File

Mnemonics can help you study and learn new information. Every time you face a new fact, ask yourself, "What does this make me think of?" For example:
The **bow** of a ship is in the front (one **bows forward**);
The **stern** and **aft** are **after** — or at the back.
Seismology is the study of earthquakes. (What is the **size** of the quake?)

30

Train Your Brain!

Does your mind go blank when you're in front of the class?

Do you forget what you've read in your textbook five minutes later? If so, use the first letters of key words, phrases, or ideas to create your own memory aids.

For example, suppose you have to give an oral report on jellyfish. You want to remember to cover the following in your talk.

—Jellyfish: Are they really fish?
—Where jellyfish live
—What they eat
—Other important details

You create the mnemonic **Fake Fish, HFC** to help you remember the order of your talk.

Fake Fish (You'll discuss how jellyfish are different from fish.)

H (You'll discuss their **h**abitat — where, how, and with whom they live)

F (F stands for **f**ood)

C (C stands for **c**haracteristics and **c**ontext — you'll give details and talk about jellyfish in relation to other ocean creatures.)

Hop Aboard the Memory Train

In the spaces below, write the spelling words or facts you want to remember. Next to each, create your own way to help you learn it.

What I Need to Remember	How I Will Remember
_____	_____
_____	_____
_____	_____
_____	_____
_____	_____

TAKE NOTE!

Good notes help you remember what you hear or read. Here are a few tips for taking notes.

Include Key Facts Only

Don't write every word. And don't write whole sentences, either. Use only phrases or single words. Abbreviate whenever you can. Here is an example.

What you read or hear: Baseball is the most popular sport in the United States.

What you write: Baseball — #1 sport in U.S.

Use Signs and Symbols

It's often faster to write a symbol instead of a word. Here are some common note-taking tricks.

Instead of	Use
and	+
the same as	=
number	#
important	*
different	≠

Review and Rewrite

Read over your notes after you write them. Be sure you understand what you have written. Rewrite them to make them clearer.

What's the Point?

When you take notes, jot down the main ideas and details. This helps you to remember and understand what you have read. Try to figure out the author's point, which ties all the information and facts together. The main idea is usually found at the end of an article or chapter.

NOTE TAKING TIDBITS

From something fishy to news of ancient Egypt, you'll probably enjoy these far-out facts as you practice your note-taking skills under each passage.

Fish that live at the bottom of the sea are in total darkness. The lantern fish has a glowing spot on its head to help it see. The light it gives off is enough to read a book by. Blindfish have rows of projections on their bodies that are sensitive to touch. They help the blindfish get around without bumping into things. Blindfish have no eyes at all!

_____

_____

_____

_____

You have to teach a dog to roll over and play dead. But "playing dead" comes naturally to opossums. When an opossum is in danger, its body becomes stiff. Most large animals eat prey they've hunted and killed themselves. If they see an opussum that appears dead they won't bother with it. The opossum waits until the larger animal has moved. Then it gets up and goes about its business.

_____

_____

_____

_____

The penguin is a bird, but it can't fly. Its feathers are more like fur. The penguin uses its wings like flippers. This helps it move in water. The penguin is the only bird that can walk upright. When not in the water, the penguin waddles around. To move quickly, it does a belly flop and uses its wing flippers to glide across the ice and snow.

_____

_____

_____

_____

Ants live in underground nests that are a lot like cities. There are roads that lead in and out. There are many workers doing many jobs. Some ants guard the city, and some care for the babies. Some hunt for food, while others grow food in ant "gardens." Ants are members of cooperative communities.

_____

_____

_____

_____

In ancient Egypt, cats were treated like royalty. Cat owners would share their own meals with their cats. They'd put gold earrings in their cats' ears. When a cat died, it was mummified and given a fancy funeral. Cat owners shaved their eyebrows to show their sorrow. Everyone mourned — everyone, that is, except the mice!

_____

_____

_____

_____

Math Homework Tips

You can do better in math without learning any more arithmetic. That's because most math mistakes are caused by carelessness, not lack of understanding. Here are some ideas to help your homework "add up" to success.

Scrap It!
Using scrap paper gives you a better chance of getting the right answer because you can review your work. Try doing the following problem in your head, then use scratch paper. Which answer do you trust?

$$472$$
$$+ \ 39$$
$$\overline{}$$

What's Your Sign?
What's the first thing you should do when you have a math problem? Look at the sign! Many people add when they should subtract and vice versa.

Keep It Straight!
Do you sometimes have trouble keeping columns of numbers straight? Here's a trick to try. Use lined paper turned sideways. That will give you neat columns in which to write. Try it.

Easy Does It.

When you have math homework, answer the easy problems first. This helps you warm up so you feel confident about tackling tougher problems.

Don't spend too much time on problems you get hung up on. Put a check next to the problem and move on. Go back to the hard problems later; if you're still stumped, ask someone for help.

Key In on Important Words.

Look for key words that tell which computation is needed, such as estimating or subtracting. Key words include: *more than, less than, between, nearest, least, greatest.*

Check It Out.

Check subtraction problems by adding; check division problems by multiplying; and check multiplication by dividing.

Think of "Fact Families" Before You Solve.

For instance, if you're trying to figure out 16–9, try remembering the name of its addition "relative": **9 + 7 = 16**. The missing number in the subtraction problem, then, must be 7! Do the same for division and multiplication, which also share common family members.

Do It the Write Way.

Write down each piece of information that is given. Write or circle what each problem asks you to find. Get your answer. Then go back and make sure it answers the question you wrote or circled.

Keep It Down and Add It Up.

Reduce fractions to their smallest parts. To compare fractions, rename them as like fractions.

Example: $\quad 3/_9 = 1/_3 \qquad\qquad 4/_8 = 1/_2$

When looking for the correct answer to a problem, look for the fraction that has been reduced.

When fractions have the same denominator, add or subtract only the numerators.

Example: $\quad 1/_5 + 2/_5 = 3/_5$

Tips for Science and Social Studies

Last Things First

When you have to read a chapter for homework, turn to the questions at the end. Read the questions before you begin the chapter. That way, you'll know ahead of time what the chapter is about and what information to look for as you read.

What Did You Say?

After you've finished reading, go back and reread just the heavy-type headings and subheadings. Turn each one into a question to review what you've read and to check whether you remember it. For example:

How Heat Moves Through Solid Matter (How does heat move through a solid?)

The Moving Ocean (How and why does the ocean move?)

The Reasons for the Civil War (What were the reasons for the Civil War?)

Texas Becomes a State (When and how did Texas become a state?)

Shape Up Your Notes.

When you take notes, picture an upside-down triangle. Think of all the facts you've read. Say to yourself: *Oh, really? So what?* to get to the point — or reason — for what you've just learned. What did the writer want you to come away understanding?

Main Idea

Details

Main Point

Table It!

Sometimes, information is given in table, graph, or chart form. Always "read" these parts of the lesson. They often show or sum up important ideas. Look for key words to help you understand what is being measured or shown.

Fact Finding

To find what chapter contains certain information, look at the table of contents. To find the pages that have certain facts, use the index at the back of the book.

Order, Order!

To understand the correct order or sequence of events, look for signal words such as *first*, *then*, *later*, *finally*, and *last*. To help you remember things in order, make a time line. Use memory aids, such as acronyms (made-up names or words using the first letters of terms you want to remember). An acronym for the colors of the spectrum is:

Red	Orange	Yellow	Green	Blue	Indigo	Violet
			Roy G. Biv			

Relationships

Many ideas and events in social studies are related by cause and effect. Key words such as *because, as a result, since, consequently,* and *so* are relationship words you should pay special attention to. You can use visual aids to keep track of events that cause other events to happen.

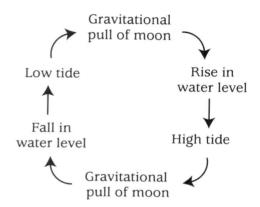

Circle In on Details.

When you study history or science, you often compare two things. Words such as *like*, *same*, *but*, *unlike*, *on the other hand*, and *however* are words that tell about comparisons. When you make comparisons, you can highlight similarities and differences by writing your notes in intersecting circles called *Venn diagrams*.

Hang-Ups!

Use index cards to help you study. Write the names of persons, events, or topics on the fronts and some related details and facts on the backs. Use clothespins to attach the cards to a jumprope "line" strung above our bed. Review a few cards each night before you go to sleep.

What Do You Think?

Your teacher may ask for an opinion or prediction. Put all the reasons for and against your opinion in a list. Then choose the most important reason to help support your opinion.

Homework Tips for Reading

What's the Story?
Figure out what kind of story you're reading by looking at the details. When does the story take place? Could this story really happen? Could the characters be real people? Watch for expressions that don't mean exactly what the words say, such as *skinny as a beanpole.*

Take It Lightly.
Skim the chapter before you start reading. Skimming means reading something through quickly by letting your eyes scan each page. You'll get an idea of what the chapter is about and will be able to read more smoothly.

Get the Picture?
There's more to reading than words. You have to "read" pictures, too. They help you understand stories and characters. Pictures and diagrams help you understand textbooks, too. Use the illustrations to help you understand what you're reading.

What's the Good Word?
In textbooks, important words often appear in heavy type. You can usually figure out what these words mean by looking at the words around them. If you still can't figure out what a word means, look in the glossary at the back of the book. A glossary is like a dictionary; it tells what a word means.

Don't Use Your Head.
Try not to move your head as you read. Let your eyes do the moving. Also, try not to move your lips as you read. All of these actions slow you down. Put your fingers on your lips as you read to keep them from moving.

No More Word for Word!
Reading words one by one in a sentence can slow you down. Instead, train your eyes to see words in groups of two or three words. Group words that go together and let your eyes look at them as a whole. To practice this, read the next tip.

Practice Makes Perfect.

Train your eyes to read word groups. Circle the words that go together in the following story.

A mouse was dancing wildly on top of a jar of jelly. Another mouse came along and asked the first mouse why it was dancing.
"Can't you read?" replied the first mouse. "It says: 'Twist to Open.'"

Stay on Top of Things.

In every sentence, passage, or paragraph some words are more important than others. The important ones are called key words. The key words give you the message. You'll read better if you concentrate just on the key words. Example:

Whole Passage: *I've been sitting on top of a flagpole for 14 days. I have broken the world's record for flagpole sitting. I will write you a long letter all about it when I come back down to earth.*

Key Words: *Been on flagpole 14 days. Broken world's record. Will write.*

Little Things Mean a Lot

Sometimes one little word can change the meaning of a whole sentence. Learn to zero in on important words.

For example:

Do your homework before you watch TV.
Do your homework while you watch TV.
Which sentence seems like more fun?

Try these:

You can get a book or candy.
You can get a book and candy.
In which sentence do you have to choose between two things?

When I go shopping, I will take you.
If I go shopping, I will take you.
In which sentence is the speaker not sure of going shopping?

Take Five

No matter what the subject, take breaks from your work every 20 minutes or so. Stretch. Walk around. Rest your eyes by focusing on a spot in the distance. Don't do homework without taking breaks. It will only tire you and cause you to make silly mistakes.

When you finish your homework, do something fun. Consider it a reward for a job well done!

TAKE A TIP FROM A KID...

To save time in the morning, plan what to wear to school the night before.

Unclutter your mind! Write everything on a calendar and keep it on your door. Check the calendar every day.

Pack your bookbag at night. In your usual morning rush, you could forget things.

Be the first to get to the library when a report is assigned so you'll have a choice of books to check out.

Give yourself more time than you think you'll need for big projects.

Save notes, handouts from your teacher, even ticket stubs from field trips to refer back to while studying!

Use a tape recorder for studying. It's a fun way to memorize things.

Know which kids to call when you're stuck on homework.

Eat right. Get enough sleep and exercise. All these will give you more energy for school.

Check the tips that work for you. Star the ones you're willing to try. Then add your own and your classmates' to the page.

My Tips _____

_____

My Classmates' Tips_____

PART 3

IMPROVING YOUR READING

Let's face it: Reading is an important part of schoolwork. Not only do you need to read textbooks to learn things; reading for pleasure is often a big part of homework.

Are you ever stuck without a good book to read? Do you waste time in the library not knowing where to look? In this section, you'll:

- take a reading inventory;
- improve your reading skills;
- learn how to write a perfect book report;
- get the scoop on questions teachers love to ask;
- see what books other kids your age are recommending.

READING INVENTORY

An important part of reading for pleasure is being able to choose the books you want to read. This fun "test" (which you can't fail) will help you pinpoint your interests.

PART 1

The funniest book I ever read: _____

My favorite author: _____

A book that made me think: _____

A book everyone should read: _____

A book I've read more than once: _____

A real scary book: _____

A book about kids like me: _____

A book my parents read to me: _____

A book all my friends are reading: _____

A book I wish I had written: _____

If I ever write a book, it will be about _____

_____

PART 2

I enjoy books about

- ❏ real life
- ❏ adventure
- ❏ famous people
- ❏ fairy tales
- ❏ myths and legends
- ❏ animals
- ❏ history
- ❏ outer space
- ❏ sports

The last two books I read were

Title: _____

Author: _____

Title: _____

Author: _____

If a friend asked me to recommend a book, I'd tell my friend to read

_____

I think this book is great because _____

_____

_____

_____

FICTION FACT SHEET

Sometimes you're expected to read a fiction book as part of a class project. When you do, you'll want to be able to remember it well enough to answer questions on a test or do a report.

Fill in the fact sheet on these pages with details from a book you're reading now. It will give you some good ideas for remembering facts for every new book you read.

Name of book _____

Author _____

Sum It Up
Tell what happens in each chapter below.

Chapter	What Happens in Chapter
_____	_____
_____	_____
_____	_____
_____	_____
_____	_____
_____	_____
_____	_____

Main Characters
Write the names and something about each character below.

Character	Kind of Person He or She Is
_____	_____
_____	_____
_____	_____

What is the most important problem the main character must solve?

_____

_____

How does the main character solve the problem?

_____

_____

_____

Note key events from the story and the pages where each event happens.

Big Event	Pages
_____	_____
_____	_____
_____	_____
_____	_____

Find pages that are important for rereading. Tell why. For instance, a page might give a good description of a character or provide an important quote.

Pages	What Happens
_____	_____
_____	_____
_____	_____

Why do you think the author wrote this book? What message is he or she trying to communicate?

_____

_____

What new words or ideas did you learn from this book?

_____

If I Were Teacher...
What would a teacher want you to remember about this book?

_____

_____

What questions would a teacher ask?

_____

_____

_____

TEACHERS' CHOICE

Teachers are always thinking of new homework ideas to help you understand the books you read. Read the list of assignments and how you can prepare for each.

Prepare a book jacket for a book you've just read.
- Study a real book jacket.
- Notice that the title and author appear on the front cover and the spine.
- Find: Where the book summary goes;
  Where information about the author appears;
  The purpose of the illustration on the front cover.

Next time I do this type of project, I'll _____

_____

Take a scene from the book and turn it into a play.
- Describe the setting.
- Prepare a brief description of each character.
- Write a conversation (dialogue) between the characters.
- Be sure to include stage directions:
  how actors say their lines;
  how actors move and where they stand;
  what props actors will hold
  These directions appear in (parentheses).

Next time I try this, I'll _____

_____

Write a book review.
- Create a headline that captures your feelings about the book.
- Write something about the author, such as his or her other books.
- Summarize the book (give the main idea) without giving away its ending.
- Give the book a rating. Include:
  the age of the person who would like it;
  the interests of the person who would like it;
  Back up your opinions with reasons and facts.

Next time I try this, I'll _____

_____

Create a poster or diorama based on your book.
- Draw or cut out models of main characters;
- Create the background setting from an important scene in the book;
- Include key objects from the story.
- Include words that describe the story (mysterious stranger, missing money, dark and gloomy night).

Next time I try this, I'll _____

_____

How to Write Your Best Book Report

If you have an old-fashioned book report to write, follow these steps.

1. Know why you like the book.

Ask yourself the following questions as you read the book.

- Does it make you laugh? If so, what makes it funny?
- Do the characters get themselves into silly or dangerous situations?
- Can you relate something in the book to something that's happened to you? Does reading about these characters help you understand yourself or others more?
- Does the book make you feel strongly about something? If so, what?
- If the book is nonfiction, are you learning about something you're really interested in?

When you're ready to do your report, you'll have plenty to write about!

2. Decide what you need to include in your report.

In most book reports, you need to describe:

- **what kind** of book it is (nonfiction, fiction, fantasy, biography);
- **the subject** of the book;
- **your feelings** about things that happened in the book.

Write one or two paragraphs for each element.

3. Write your first draft.

First Paragraph

Suppose you read a nonfiction book about popcorn. Here's how your first paragraph might read:

> The Popcorn Book *by Tomie de Paola is a nonfiction book that tells all about popcorn. The book explains when popcorn was discovered and who discovered it. It also explains how popcorn kernels pop, why it is a favorite snack, and how to make popcorn.*

Second Paragraph

In your second paragraph, give more detail about the book. For example, you might relate some amazing facts about popcorn for *The Popcorn Book,* above. Here's an example from a fiction book:

> Aldo Applesauce *by Joanna Hurwitz is a funny book about a fourth-grade boy who moves to a new town and has trouble making friends. The only person who is nice to him is DeDe, an unusual girl who wears a fake mustache to school!*

If you read a biography, your report might begin like this:

The Story of Thomas Alva Edison, Inventor by Margaret Davidson *is a true story. The book tells about Tom Edison's life, from his birth to his death. It tells about how he invented the electric light, movies, and the phonograph. It tells about all his inventions.*

Third Paragraph

Write what the author's message might be. To understand the author's message, ask yourself: Why did the author write this book? What meaning did he or she want readers to get?

One shortcut is to ask yourself what the main character learned. Did the main character change in any way as a result of the events of the story? Does the main character look at things differently at the end of the book?

Last Paragraph

The conclusion of your book report tells what you think of the book. Knowing whether you liked or disliked a book is simple. Explaining why is a little harder.

Think back to step 1–the questions you asked yourself as you were reading. Once you've listed a few reasons for your opinion, give examples from the book to back them up.

4. Finishing Touches

Decide:

Is the report too long or too short?

Does it say exactly what I mean?

Will my audience understand what I'm saying?

Ask someone to read your report aloud to you. Listening to your own report is a good way to catch and fix something that you didn't pick up when you read it to yourself.

5. Rewriting

Before you copy your report over, check spelling and punctuation. Write or type it neatly.

WRITE HERE NOW

Introduction

For my book report I've chosen _____

written by _____

This is a (circle one) fiction / nonfiction book which is about

_____

_____

Give details

For fiction, tell about characters and plot; for nonfiction, mention some of the topics the book explores. The book _____

_____

_____

_____

Author's message

I think the point the author was trying to get across through this book is

_____

_____

_____

_____

Personal feelings about book

I really liked this book because

_____

I really disliked this book because

_____

The book made me feel

_____

People who would most like this book are

_____

_____

Summary

In conclusion, I think that _____

_____

_____

TRY IT!

Think of a book you've just read or are still reading. Then follow the guided paragraphs on page 50 to write a first draft below.

_____

_____

_____

_____

_____

_____

_____

_____

_____

_____

_____

_____

_____

_____

_____

_____

_____

_____

_____

_____

_____

_____

_____

_____

_____

_____

_____

SPEAK UP!

Some teachers assign oral book reports. That means they'll expect you to read your report or talk about your book in front of the class. Whether you memorize your book report or read from a written report, you'll need to practice. Practice reading aloud in front of a mirror, in front of a family member, or even in front of a pet!

If you choose to speak about your book instead of reading your report aloud, you'll want to jot down a few important points about your book on index cards. Print clearly in large letters so you can read your cards with just a quick glance.

For practice, fill in the cards below with a few main points about your book. Whichever you choose, speak slowly. Speak clearly. Make eye contact with your audience. Be yourself. Remember: You know better than anyone else what you plan to say.

KID PICKS

These books are very popular with kids your age. So the next time you have a book report coming up or you simply want a good book to read, consider one of these.

Anastasia Krupnik by Lois Lowry
Otherwise Known as Sheila the Great by Judy Blume
Baseball in April by Gary Soto
Blue Willow by Doris Gates
Bridge to Terabithia by Katherine Paterson
Chocolate Fever by Robert Kimmel Smith
The Cricket in Times Square by George Selden
Danny the Champion of the World by Roald Dahl
Dear Mr. Henshaw by Beverly Cleary
Einstein Anderson, Science Sleuth by Seymour Simon
Every Living Thing by Cynthia Rylant
From the Mixed-up Files of Mrs. Basil E. Frankweiler written
        and illustrated by E. L. Konigsburg
Getting Something on Maggie Marmelstein by Marjorie Weinman Sharmat
How to Eat Fried Worms by Thomas Rockwell
Howliday Inn by James Howe
Indian in the Cupboard by Lynne Reid Banks
Island of the Blue Dophins by Scott O'Dell
A Jar of Dreams by Yoshiko Uchida
Julie of the Wolves by Jean Craighead George
The Night Journey by Kathryn Lasky
The People Could Fly by Virginia Hamilton
Philip Hall Likes Me, I Reckon Maybe by Bette Greene
Prairie Songs by Pam Conrad
Sarah, Plain and Tall and *Skylark* by Patricia MacLachlan
*Scary Stories to Tell in the Dark: Collected from
        American Folklore* by Alvin Schwartz
Sign of the Beaver by Elizabeth George Speare
The Trumpet of the Swan by E. B. White
Tuck Everlasting by Natalie Babbitt
A Wrinkle in Time by Madeleine L'Engle

AUTHOR, AUTHOR!

Most of the authors on the Kid Picks list have written several books. So once you've found a book you like, look for others by that same author.

READING LOGS

Here's your chance to "log in." Use the sample Reading Logs provided here to record your ideas. (You may want to make a few copies of these sheets before you start filling them in.) Rate and date each book you finish and write a few comments about it.

Title of Book: _____

Author: _____

Date Completed: _____

Comment: _____

Rating: Super!   Good   So-so   Not so good

Title of Book: _____

Author: _____

Date Completed: _____

Comment: _____

Rating: Super!   Good   So-so   Not so good

Title of Book: _____

Author: _____

Date Completed: _____

Comment: _____

Rating: Super!   Good   So-so   Not so good

Title of Book: _____

Author: _____

Date Completed: _____

Comment: _____

Rating: Super!   Good   So-so   Not so good

Title of Book: _____

Author: _____

Date Completed: _____

Comment: _____

Rating: Super!   Good   So-so   Not so good

Title of Book: _____

Author: _____

Date Completed: _____

Comment: _____

Rating: Super!   Good   So-so   Not so good

WHAT'S THE GOOD WORD?

The more you read, the more new words you will learn. Jot down any unfamiliar words you come across in your reading. Note how the words are used and guess their meanings. Later, look up the words in the dictionary. (You may want to make several copies of this page, too!)

WORD	HOW USED?	MY GUESS	ACTUAL MEANING

PART 4

IMPROVING YOUR WRITING

How do you decide what to write about?
What makes a good research topic?
How do you find and organize information?
What makes a paper interesting?
These are some of the questions this section
will help you answer. When you're done,
you'll feel more confident about sharing
your thoughts on paper.

WRITE AT THE BEGINNING

The best way to start writing is to jump right in. This is not the time to organize your thoughts into tidy categories. It's the time to brainstorm — to tap into ideas, images, memories, and so on.

Many writers find that a web or sunburst is a useful way to get started. Here's how you fill one in:
- **In the center of the web, indicate the topic you want to write about.**
- **Fill in the other spaces with ideas that "pop" into your head related to that topic.**

Try it. Think of a topic that interests you. Then let your mind go. Think of as many related ideas as you can.

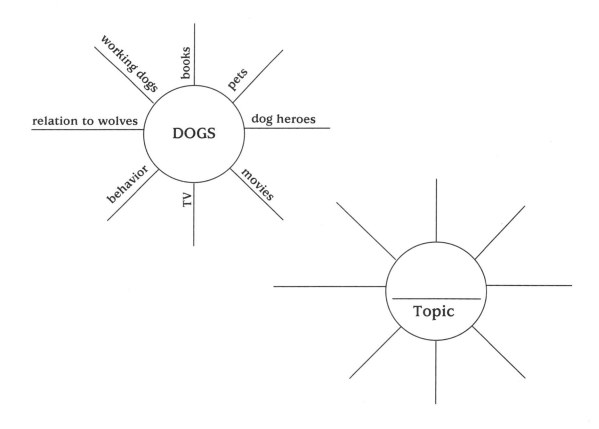

RECIPE FOR WRITING SUCCESS

When you cook, you follow steps in a recipe. When you write, you also follow steps or stages. Here they are.

STEP 1: Prewriting

Write about what you know.
It's easier to write about something you know. Draw on your own experiences to come up with ideas.

Scout around.
Be on the lookout for good material to write about. Get a little notepad and jot down ideas as they occur to you. Something you read or see on TV may trigger an idea for writing.

Write every day.
Keep a diary or journal. This helps you train yourself to become comfortable writing and to zero in on your own experiences.

Narrow your topic.
Focus on one part of a larger subject. For instance, instead of writing about the whole Olympics, try focusing on a particular event or athlete.

Sort things out.
Decide what details you'll cover before you write. Group ideas to come up with an overall main idea.

STEP 2: Getting it Down

Be bold.
Your opening line will tell what your paper is about. Try to think of an introduction that grabs the reader's attention. For instance: If you think jellyfish are fish, guess again!

Let details be your guide.
Your opening sets the tone and direction of your paper. Use your groups of details to develop the sentences and paragraphs that follow. Each paragraph should introduce a new idea or group of details.

Sum it up.

Your ending will repeat the main idea of your paper in different words. Sometimes the best way to wrap up a paper is to go back to the beginning. Suppose you opened a paper about pollution this way: Imagine day after day without sunshine. After building a case for cutting back on pollution, your closing could be: If we don't clean up our planet, we will be doomed to live in darkness forever.

Cap it off.

Most people prefer to create a title for their story or article after they're done with the main body of text. Like a newspaper headline, titles should grab the reader's attention and, in a few words, describe what your paper is about.

STEP 3: Revising and Editing

Polish it up.

Reread your paper a few times to yourself:

How does it sound?

Do all your ideas hang together?

Have you chosen the best words to say what you want?

Rewrite your paper until it reads "just right."

Be an editor.

Now you're ready to proofread to catch all those spelling mistakes, incomplete or run-on sentences, and awkward descriptions. Language textbooks usually provide excellent editing checklists that'll help make changes.

STEP 4: Rewriting

Finish with a flourish.

Copy or type your final paper. Remember: Like it or not, teachers prefer papers that are neat. After all, that usually does make them easier to read. Be sure to spiff up and staple in any diagrams or illustrations you might want to include.

Take the credit.

Before you hand in your paper, be sure to put your name and date on it. After all, you deserve to be recognized for a job well done!

Oops!

When you're working on your first draft, write on every third line. This way, you'll have plenty of space to make corrections and rewrite. Take a break between finishing your rough draft and beginning your final paper.

For fun, proofread your work by using the same symbols real editors use.

PROOFREADER'S SYMBOL	WHAT SYMBOL MEANS
ℒ	take out (delete)
∧	insert (put in)
≡	capitalize
⁋	new paragraph
⊙	period
⋀	put in comma
stet	let it stay
⌒	close up, no extra space
∿	fix order of letters
⋎"	insert quotation marks
⋎	put in apostrophe

MAIL CALL: WRITING LETTERS

Friendly letters are just what they sound like—letters between friends or relatives. You don't have to put the addresses on the letters into any special form. But for business letters, which you may be sending to people you don't know, addresses must be written in a specific form.

All letters have these parts:

Heading
The heading includes your address, the date and, in a business letter, the name and address of the person to whom you are writing.

Greeting
The greeting generally begins with *Dear* and the name of the person you are writing. In a friendly letter, the name is followed by a comma. In a business letter, the name is followed by a colon. Don't forget to capitalize each word in a greeting.

Body
This is the main part of your letter. You may want to indent every paragraph.

Closing
Use formal closings, like *Yours truly* or *Sincerely,* in a business letter. In a personal letter, the closing word could be *Love, Your Friend,* or whatever you choose.

Remember to capitalize the first word in the closing and put a comma at the end of the closing.

Signature
Sign your name underneath the closing. In a formal letter, type or print your name beneath your signature.

BUSINESS LETTER

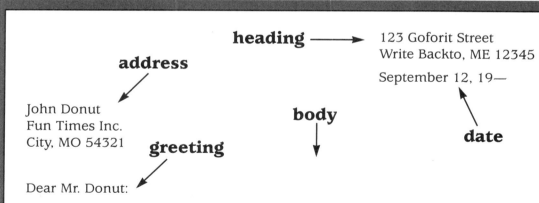

heading ⟶ 123 Goforit Street
Write Backto, ME 12345

September 12, 19—

address ↙

John Donut
Fun Times Inc.
City, MO 54321

greeting ↘

body ↓

date ↖

Dear Mr. Donut:

Your ad to get a "round tuit" was very clever. I ordered one three months ago to give as a gift. Well, I just received it. It's too late now. My friend's birthday came and went. I am returning the tuit, along with my sales receipt, and expect a full refund. A word of advice: The next time you receive an order, you should get a "round tuit" yourself a lot faster!

closing ⟶ Sincerely,

signature ⟶ Ima Madd

ENVELOPE

Your name
Your address

return address

Cliff Hanger
321 Mountain Avenue
Great Falls, MO 54321

**name and address of person
receiving letter**

Place
Stamp
Here

FRIENDLY LETTER

July 4, 19—

Dear Pat,
This place is here.
Wish you were beautiful.
Just kidding,

Matt

TOOLS OF THE TRADE: OUTLINES

Many writers plan research papers by first making an outline. An outline is the same thing to a writer as a rough sketch is to an artist. It gives a step-by-step plan for reaching a certain goal.

An outline helps you develop a beginning, middle, and ending for your paper. It also helps you organize your details into main headings and subheadings. Here's an outline for a report on Sojourner Truth.

SOJOURNER TRUTH (1797-1883)

I. Childhood
    A. Born in New York
    B. Born a slave
    C. Real name Isabelle Hardenbergh (called Belle)
    D. Sold from mother at age 9

II. Adulthood
    A. Had three children
    B. Freed in 1827
    C. Named self
        1. Sojourner means wanderer
        2. Truth for a way to live
    D. Died at age 87

III. Accomplishments
    A. Gave speeches against slavery
    B. Worked for Women's Rights
    C. Met with President Abraham Lincoln
    D. Addressed Congress after Civil War

This outline gives you a good idea of how to organize a report about a person. Break down the person's life into sections. (For example: Childhood, Adulthood, Later years, Accomplishments)

OUTLINE WORKSHEET

Skeletons Make Great Ghostwriters!

Outlines are often called *skeletons* because they contain just the bare bones of a paper. To practice making your own outline, first make copies of this page. Then fill in the blanks with details about your topic.

My Topic:

Overall Main Idea:

I.
    A.
        1.
        2.
    B.
        1.
        2.
            a.
            b.

II.

THE TIMES OF YOUR LIFE

Sometimes a time line can be a useful part of a report, especially when you're telling about a famous person. A time line doesn't show every year that a person lived, just the years when interesting or important things happened in that person's life.

Just for fun, prepare a time line about yourself in the space below. Because you're still alive (more or less), your time line just continues into the future with no ending date.

First, jot down some key events and dates from your own life. Examples you may want to highlight include the year you

- were born;
- started school;
- got a dog;
- learned to read;
- got a baby brother or sister.

Write events in the spaces next to the years when they happened. If the date falls between one of the years marked below, write about where it would belong on the line. For an extra special touch, add drawings or photos to your time line.

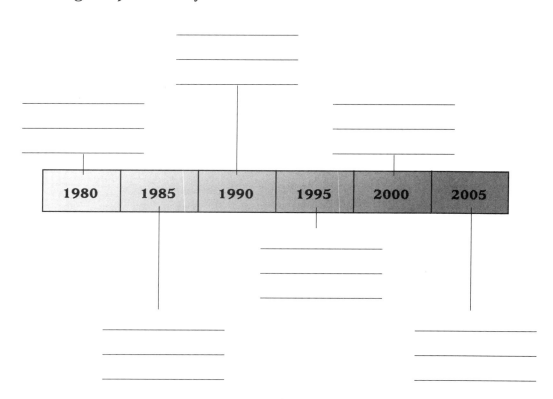

WHAT'S THE STORY?

If you're writing a story or play, you don't absolutely need an outline. But it helps. Here's one way to get a story in shape.

Story title: _____

Characters:_____

Setting (time and place): _____

Problem or challenges main characters face: _____

Major events in the story: _____

Story ending (how the problems are worked out): _____

_____

_____

_____

_____

_____

_____

_____

_____

_____

BE A POET!

When you're challenged to write a poem for school, it's usually one with a special rhyme or form. Here are a few popular ones.

Limerick
A limerick is a short, silly poem written in five lines.
Lines **1, 2,** and **5** rhyme.
These are the longest lines, with five to seven beats.
Lines **3** and **4** rhyme.
Say the following limerick out loud a few times to get the swing of it.

> *There once was a barber named Stu*
> *Who worked very hard at the zoo.*
> *He was very brave*
> *To give lions a shave.*
> *And to give the brown bear a shampoo.*

Haiku
A haiku is a three-line poem. Each line has a certain number of beats, or syllables.
Line One has **5** syllables
Line Two has **7** syllables
Line Three has **5** syllables
Here is an example:

> *The huge sea gull sails*
> *Over the beach and ocean*
> *Swooping down to snack.*

Tanka
A tanka poem starts off like a haiku, but it is two lines longer. The last two lines have **7** syllables each. Here is an example:

> *I like you a lot.*
> *So I wrote this rhyme for you,*
> *Put it on your desk,*
> *And watched in horror as the*
> *Teacher read it to the class!*

© 1996 Good Apple

Name Poem

A name poem is a good way to introduce yourself or write about someone you know. Each line begins with a letter of the name. Example:

RACHEL
Real good sense of humor
Always wears jeans
Competitive swimmer
Hates early morning wake ups
Enjoys singing
Loves dog Max

GO FOR IT!

Choose one type of poem to write on the lines.

_____

_____

_____

_____

_____

_____

_____

_____

_____

_____

_____

_____

_____

_____

_____

_____

WRITING AN ESSAY

Do you have strong feelings about pollution or why recess should be longer? Strong feelings about a particular topic are called your point-of-view, or *opinion.*

An essay is simply the type of writing in which you state your opinion. To write a really good essay, you have to back up your opinion with details ("Recess is only 15 minutes.") and examples ("If recess was an hour, we could all get more exercise.").

Think of a topic you feel strongly about or choose one from the list that follows. Then use the practice form on this page as a model for writing. (You may want to make copies of the page first before filling it in.)

Save the Rain Forests
Raise (or Lower) the Voting Age
Get Rid of Summer Vacation: Why School Should Be Year-round
Lengthen (or Shorten) the School Day
No More Grading!
What Students Should Learn in Middle School
Why It Is (or Isn't) Important to Learn a Second Language

Something I believe strongly about is _____

_____

One reason I believe this is _____

_____

Another reason is _____

_____

An example that proves this point is _____

_____

I strongly feel that _____

_____

In closing, let me say that _____

_____

WHAT'S NEWS?

News stories are real-life accounts of events. A news story answers the questions *who, what, when, where, how,* and sometimes *why.* When you write a news story, think of a triangle.

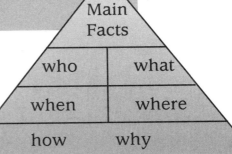

Begin with just the main facts. As you continue, your story triangle widens as you fill in the details of the facts you stated up front. Every news story has the following parts.

Headline

The headline is usually a catchy title that tells what the story will be about.

Lead

The lead is the first sentence or paragraph of the news story. It grabs the readers' interest and tells the basic facts of the story.

Body

The body fills in the details about the lead.

Read the example of a headline and lead below. Use what you know about the story to write the body of the news article.

Writing a News Story

1. Get the Facts.

- Gather as much information as possible.
- Interview people who were involved.
- Find experts to talk about what happened.
- Take notes. Be sure to get the exact words of the people you will quote.

You'll know you have enough information to write a good news story if you can answer the five questions: Who, What, When, Where, How/Why.

2. Write the lead.

Tell the basic facts of the story. Try to get the readers interested.

3. Body build.

Fill in the details given in the lead.

4. Write a headline.

Try to think of a catchy headline that sums up the main idea of the article.

Prince Seeks Owner of Glass Slipper

Last night at the Royal Ball, Prince Charming was swept off his feet by a mystery woman who suddenly fled at the stroke of midnight. The only clue to her identity was the single glass slipper she dropped on her way out. "I will not rest until I find the foot that fits this shoe," announced the Prince early this morning.

BE A REPORTER

Think of an event happening in your school. Use the space on the next page to write your news story.

EXTRA! EXTRA! READ ALL ABOUT IT!

School News

Letters to the Editor

Use the space that follows to write a letter to the editor expressing a personal opinion about something.

TAKE A TIP FROM A KID...

Before you do homework, write down exactly what you have to do. Estimate how long each part will take.

Your schoolwork, like the way you dress, represents who you are. Take it seriously if you want people to take you seriously.

If you want to remember something, like a spelling word, write it over and over again.

Find magazines and books on the same topics you're studying in school. They can offer interesting new information and are more fun to read than textbooks!

When you write, put things in your own words. Your reports will be more interesting that way.

If you cheat, you'll lose the respect of other kids.

Get help if you don't understand something. Things get worse if you keep pretending everything is fine.

Don't be afraid to make mistakes. Even grown-ups learn from mistakes!

Make a list of all the reasons you want to do better in school. Keep yourself motivated by reading your list every few days.

Check the tips that work for you. Star the ones you plan to try. Add your own tips and classmates' tips.

Here's a good tip of mine that works: _____

_____

Here's a tip from a classmate: _____

_____

RESEARCH PAPERS

You have to track down information for a research paper. Most often, you will use your school or public library to find material on your topic. In the past, you'd look up information about books in a card catalog, a kind of filing cabinet. You'd look for **title, author,** or **subject** cards that were filed alphabetically in the drawers.

Today, most libraries store information about books and magazines in a computer. In most instances, you click on "View catalog" to start your search. Then you choose title, author, or subject. (You click on "Search periodicals" when you want to find a magazine article.)

You can scroll down the list of books that appear on the screen until you spot the one that seems right for you. The profile of the book includes a line that reads something like this:

Location: HTS JUV. 551.46 G (J Book)
This "location line" tells you where in the library to look for the book. In the case above, the book can be found in the juvenile or children's section of the Hastings Public Library. (The letters JUV stand for "juvenile.") The call number 551.46 G tells where to look on the shelf.

Thanks, Mr. Dewey!

```
PIC            CROCODILES–FICTION
WAB               Waber, Bernard
FUN
                Funny, Funny Lyle/
              by Bernard Waber--1st--
           Boston: Houghton Mifflin, 1987
                   [38] pp:ill
                        ISBN 0–395–43619–2

       O  1. Crocodiles • Fic • 2. Title  O
```

The call numbers on nonfiction books are a kind of code. In 1876, librarian Melvil Dewey thought of a way to organize books. He divided nonfiction books into 10 main groups and gave each group a set of numbers. For example, science books fall between 500 and 599. History, geography, and biography books have numbers between 900 and 999.

© 1996 Good Apple

REFERENCE BOOKS

References are books and other materials people refer to for information. References are kept in a special section in the library. Unlike other books, reference books cannot be borrowed from the library. Here are some common references.

CURRENT NEWS ON FILE:
an index to newspaper articles

DICTIONARY:
a book that gives the spelling, meaning, and pronunciation of words

ALMANAC:
a book with up-to-date information on many subjects, from sports statistics to weather to important recent events

BIOGRAPHICAL DICTIONARY:
a book that gives facts about famous people

ATLAS:
a book of maps

THESAURUS:
a dictionary of synonyms and antonyms (words with same and opposite meanings)

ENCYCLOPEDIA:
a set of books with facts on many subjects

LOOK IT UP!

For practice, tell which reference you'd use to find the answer to each question. (In some cases, you could find the answer in more than one source.)

Source

1. How do you pronounce the word *phoneme?* _____

2. Is Helen of Troy a real person? _____

3. Which magazines had articles about *pogs* last year? _____

4. Which actors got Academy Awards in 1995? _____

5. What are two facts about *mako sharks?* _____

6. How far is San Diego from San Francisco? _____

7. Where is the Indian Ocean? _____

8. What word means the same as *tremble?* _____

9. What rock group had the number one song last year? _____

10. What were some names of recent hurricanes? _____

11. Is *Florence Nightingale* a type of bird? _____

12. Was James A. Garfield a U.S. president or cartoon character? _____

FACTS ON FILE

When you do a report, you need to refer to at least three sources of information. Give each source a number. When you take notes, write the number of the source next to each fact you write. Why not become an expert on a topic that interests you?

- Write your topic (heading) in the middle square.
- Write four important topics related to the main topic in the other shapes.
- Find three sources (books, encyclopedias, magazines) that contain information about your topic.
- Write facts from each source in the shapes.
- Put the number of each source next to each fact you write.

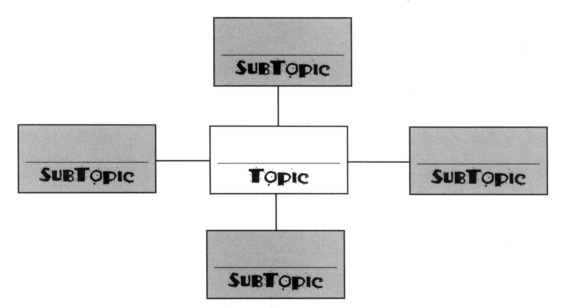

Source 1:

Title: _____

_____

Author: _____

Volume: _____

Page: _____

Publisher: _____

Copyright: _____

Source 2:

Title: _____

_____

Author: _____

Volume: _____

Page: _____

Publisher: _____

Copyright: _____

Source 3:

Title: _____

_____

Author: _____

Volume: _____

Page: _____

Publisher: _____

Copyright: _____

WRITING A BIBLIOGRAPHY

The last page of a report usually lists the sources you used to write your report. This is called the bibliography.

- Arrange books and magazine articles in alphabetical order by author.
- Give the name of the book publisher or the name of the magazine where you found the information.
- Include the date when the book or magazine was published.

To List a Book:
McGovern, Ann. *Shark Lady: True Adventures of Eugenie Clark*. Scholastic, 1978.

To List a Magazine Article:
Vitton, Elizabeth A. "Kid Ventriloquists (and Their Dummies) Have Lots To Say!" *3-2-1 Contact*, September 1994, pp. 20–23.

To List an Encyclopedia Article:
The Kingfisher Children's Encyclopedia, 1992 edition, "Milky Way."

To List a Newspaper Article:
"Chinese Skater Glides to World Title." *New York Times*, 12 March 1995, sec. 8, p. 4.

To List an Interview:
Judy Blume, Simon & Schuster, Parsippany, New Jersey. Interview, 17 January 1996.

CHECK IT OUT

Write *T* for True or *F* for False next to each statement below.

_____ Magazine and newspaper entries give the pages on which the information was found.

_____ The copyright or date of publication is always given.

_____ In writing a bibliography, the author's first name comes first.

_____ Always underline titles of books, magazines, encyclopedias, and newspapers.

_____ Titles of articles are underlined.

RESEARCH PAPER CHECKLIST

It takes time to do a research paper from beginning to end. Use the schedule on this page as a guide for doing a school report. Estimate how long it will take you to do each job. Then check off each task you complete.

Research Paper Due Date _____

Part 1: Gathering Information			
Task	**Estimated Time**	**Start Date**	**Completed**
Choose topic.	_____	_____	_____
Go to library.	_____	_____	_____
Begin research.	_____	_____	_____
List sources found.	_____	_____	_____
Assign numbers.	_____	_____	_____
Write bibliography entries for them.	_____	_____	_____
Take notes on each source.	_____	_____	_____
Sum up the main idea of your paper.	_____	_____	_____

Part 2: Organizing Your Research

Task	Estimated Time	Start Date	Completed
Read your notes and decide which info to keep or leave out.	_____	_____	_____
Arrange your notes in a logical order.	_____	_____	_____
Write an outline based on your notes.	_____	_____	_____

Part 3: Writing Your Paper

Task	Estimated Time	Start Date	Completed
Write a rough draft.	_____	_____	_____
Revise, edit, polish.	_____	_____	_____
Rewrite rough draft into final copy.	_____	_____	_____
Proofread and submit on due date.	_____	_____	_____

PART 5

IMPROVING YOUR STUDY AND TEST-TAKING SKILLS

Yikes! Your teacher just
announced a test . . .
Relax.
Once you've developed a system for
studying, you'll have nothing to fear.

In this section, you'll learn how to study
and you'll pick up textbook tips and ideas
for scoring higher on all types of tests.

WHAT'S YOUR TEST I.Q.?

"Were the questions on the test hard?"

"No, but the answers were!"

A big part of doing well in school is knowing how to take tests. To find out how good you already are at test-taking, take this test!

		Yes	No
1.	I find out ahead of time what will be on the test.		
2.	I bring to class everything I need for the test (such as number 2 pencils).		
3.	I listen to the teacher's directions.		
4.	I know how long the test will be, how many questions there are, and so on.		
5.	I write my name and date on the test paper.		
6.	I skim the whole test to see what will be expected.		
7.	I read directions carefully before doing anything.		
8.	I figure out how much time I have for each part.		
9.	I answer the easy questions first. If I have time, I go back and answer questions I skipped.		
10.	I double-check my answers.		
11.	I make sure I did every section I was supposed to.		

Look back at your answers. The more *yes* answers you have, the better prepared you are for test-taking. Write your plan for changing your *no* answers to *yes*, below.

_____

_____

TAKE A TIP FROM A KID...

When you study, reread what you want to remember. Keep rereading until you can "see" it in your mind.

Make sure you understand first what you want to memorize.

Write down page numbers and sections you don't understand. Ask someone to explain those sections to you.

You'll remember more if you look at your teacher when he or she speaks. And you won't be distracted by the kids around you.

Look at the table of contents whenever you get a new textbook. This will tell you what the whole book — and year — will be about. Then when you do each individual chapter assignment, you'll know how it fits with the big scheme of things.

Look over old tests and homework assignments when you study.

If you find your textbook hard to understand, go to the library and take out a simpler book on the subject.

Check the tips you follow yourself. Star the ones you'd like to try. Then write any tips you or classmates have on the topic of studying.

_____

_____

STUDY TIPS

You may have your own system for studying. But here's a five-step method that was developed at a university. It's called SQ3R for short. Can you guess why?

Step 1: Survey
Skim the material to get an overall picture of what you are going to study before you zoom in on the details. Before reading a textbook chapter

- look over the headings;
- note special terms that appear in dark bold type or in italics;
- examine charts, maps, and graphs.

Step 2: Question
Write down or make a mental note of questions you have about the material before you begin studying it. *Who, what, where, when, why,* and *how* are good question-starters.

Steps 3, 4, 5: Read, Recite, Review
As you read, stop frequently to recall what you've just read. Reread anything you don't understand. See if you can summarize in your own words what you have just studied.

TRY IT!
Here's a short paragraph that will help you practice using SQ3R. Before you actually read the paragraph, skim it to get an idea of what it's about. Write your guess on the first line. Then read the paragraph and complete the rest of the items.

A laser is a beam of light. It is not the same beam of light as from a flashlight, though. The light from a flashlight scatters, or moves in every direction. The light from a laser moves in just one direction. That's why a laser is so strong.

1. This paragraph is about _____

2. Two questions this paragraph answers are_____

3. Here's a summary of the paragraph in my own words: _____
_____

"SEE" WHAT YOU KNOW

KWL Chart

The letters stand for the following:

- list what you **know**,
- list what you **want to know**,
- list what you have **learned**.

This technique helps you pinpoint main ideas, recall important terms, and organize the material you've studied in a way that's easier to remember.

K	W	L
A bat has wings and flies.	How is a bat different from birds?	Birds are cold-blooded. Bats are mammals.

Venn Diagram

These intersecting circles help you compare two people or things. In the center — where the circles intersect — list everything the two have in common. In the outside spaces, write the separate characteristics of each.

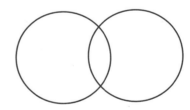

Side-by-Side Charts

This is a good way to keep track of problems and solutions, causes and effects, and so on. After you put information in this format, reread it and try to picture the charts in your head.

Cause
The temperature dropped.

Effect
The water in the birdbath froze.

Do It Yourself!

Play Jeopardy

Get a stack of index cards. On one side of each card write an important fact (name, date, event, and so on). On the other side write the matching question for that fact. Now you can review alone or work with a friend. Play Brain Quest by asking each other questions. Reverse and review the information Jeopardy-style. Give each other answers and see if you can guess the right questions.

Take Note and Question

Look through your text or class notes. Turn important facts into questions. Pretend you are making up the actual class test. Chances are, you'll be noting all the important material.

Easy Essay Practice

Review each section of your textbook and think of the main idea. Turn that main idea into a question and write it on an index card. Later, answer the question out loud or on paper.

Keep Talking

Instead of answering questions in your head, tape record your answers. Play the tape a few times as an additional way to review the material. On the back side of the tape prepare questions. Leave pauses in the recording to allow time for your answers.

Outline

Group main ideas and details in outline format. Use the dark type headings of your text as the main headings of your outline. Fill in the letter and number sections with details and supporting details. Use the blank outline that appears on page 65 of this book.

    I.
        A.
        B.
            1.
            2.

Trip Down Memory Lane

Use memory tricks you know to study for a test. For example, make a time line of important dates and events to remember. Picture the events happening, in order, in your head.

Picture Cues

Look over study aids such as Venn diagrams or charts. Reread them and picture them in your head. Write down, reread, or say out loud anything you want to remember.

CHAPTER CAPTOR!

Make copies of this page before you use it to review for a test.

Chapter or Topic of Study: _____

KNOW	WANT TO KNOW	LEARNED

TAKE A TIP FROM A KID...

Have someone in your family "quiz" you after you've studied.

Think of the questions the teacher will probably ask. Answer them in your head.

Before you read a chapter in a textbook, look at the questions at the back. The questions tell what important ideas to look for when you read.

After you've read a chapter, reread all the headings and subheadings in black type. You'll find that they sum up the key points of the chapter.

When you finish a chapter in a book, ask yourself: What were the three most important things that just happened? Say the answers in your head. Do this when you read a textbook, too.

Study with a friend and ask each other questions.

Don't stay up late cramming. You'll be in bad shape on test day. Do major studying ahead of time. Study for 15 minutes at a time, then take a break. Save the night before a test for just reviewing notes.

Check the tips that you follow. Star the ones you think you will try. Add your own and your classmates' tips on studying below.

One tip that always works for me is_____.

One tip from a classmate is _____.

THE NO-SWEAT GUIDE TO TEST TAKING

Do you have a test coming up? Not to worry. Do your studying and follow the tips below. No doubt about it. You'll do just fine. (Remember to get a good night's sleep before any exam.)

Tips to Remember

1. **Never jump right into a test.** Take your time getting started. Read the directions twice. Underline important words that tell what to do.

2. **Know how much time you have and how many points each section is worth to budget your time.** Give yourself more time for sections worth more points, such as essay questions.

3. **Do the easiest questions first.** Skip the hard ones. Put a mark in the margin next to the ones you skip, so you'll be able to go back to them.

4. **Narrow down multiple choice questions by first crossing out the obvious wrong choices.** Look for clues in other questions or in the surrounding information.

5. **Underline key words such as *true, false, largest*.** Remember that the word *not* can change the meaning of a whole statement. Remember, too, that words such as *always* and *never* usually indicate a wrong choice. But words like *frequently*, *usually*, and *sometimes* often appear in correct answers.

6. **Always save a few minutes to look over your paper when you're finished.** Make sure your name is on it. Make sure you did all you were supposed to. Review your answers, but fight the urge to go changing things too much. (If you knew an answer right away, it's probably correct.)

POP QUIZ!

Reread the six tips above. This is the second time you've seen them. How many can you remember? Close the book and test yourself.

MATH MATTERS

For example: which unit of measurement will give you a person's weight?

a) liter   b) meter   c) gram   d) kilogram

In the example, the word weight is your clue. This lets you know that you should look for a unit of weight in the answer choices.

Geometric Figures

There are two kinds of figures — those that are flat or plane and those that are solid. Can you tell them apart? Write solid or plane under each figure.

  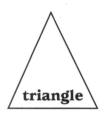

sphere   square   cone   triangle

_____   _____   _____   _____

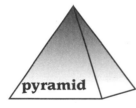 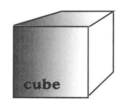 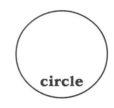

pyramid   cube   circle

_____   _____   _____

Measure for Measure

Practice geometry skills at home. Identify objects around the house by shape. Measure the **perimeter** and **area** of each room. REMEMBER: the perimeter of a shape is the length around, or the sum of all its sides (side + side + side + side = the perimeter of a rectangle).

The area of a shape is the space that shape takes up. It is usually given in square units (sq. in., sq. ft., sq. cm.). To find the area, multiply length x width (side x side).

Fractions and Decimals Add Up

The top number in a fraction is its **numerator**; the number on the bottom is the **denominator**. When fractions have the same denominators, you just add or subtract the numerators. When you work with decimals, be sure to line up the numbers so the decimal points are right under each other. Then add or subtract as you would with whole numbers.

SHORT-ANSWER TESTS

Read this page to improve at ___ .
a) bike-riding   b) singing   c) test-taking

Fill-ins. Multiple choice. Matching. True/False. These are examples of short-answer test items. They require a very simple response on your part. Here are some tips for doing your best on each kind of test.

Matching

- Work with one column at a time.
- Cross off the items you use as you go along.
- Match items that go together, such as events and dates or words and definitions. You can practice for this type of test by making up flash cards to study. Write words on one side; definitions on the other side, and so on.

True/False

- Your first hunch is usually right.
- If one part of a true/false statement is false, the whole statement is false.
- If you are not sure if a statement is true, ask yourself: Is the opposite false?
- Underline key words in each statement. Be wary of words such as *always*, *never*, *all*. Remember: on this type of item, you have a 50-50 chance of being right. So if you are unsure of an answer, take a guess anyway!

Fill-In

- Answer the item in your head first, then look for an answer that is closest to yours.
- Look for words that fit grammatically in the sentence.
- Do the easiest ones first.
- Narrow down choices by eliminating obvious wrong answers. Then read the statement to yourself with each answer that remains. Choose the one that sounds right.

Multiple Choice

- Try answering the question before looking at the choices. Then choose the choice that is closest to your answer.
- Underline key words. Cross out obvious wrong answers. Go for the best choice that remains.

Short Answer Questions

Sometimes you must provide your own answer to a question.
- Remember to answer short-answer questions in complete sentences.
- It's a good idea to repeat the question in your phrasing of the answer. For example:
  Test Item: Give one good reason for studying.
  Answer: One good reason for studying is to pass the test!

© 1996 Good Apple

91

STANDARDIZED TESTS

"Did you get the one about the roof?"

"No, it was over my head."

Schools all over the country give certain tests to check how well students are learning. These tests often come with a test booklet and a separate answer sheet. You have to pencil in tiny boxes on the answer sheet. Tests like these are called *standardized tests*.

You can't study for these tests, but you can become more familiar with how to take them.

PART 1: Sentence Sense
You are given scrambled words and are asked to make a sentence.

> **TIP**: Look at the scrambled sentence for a few seconds. Sometimes the right order will just come to you. If not, find the action word — or verb. Then find the word or phrase that tells who or what did the action. This is the subject. Put the subject before the verb. Fit the rest of the words where they belong.

For practice:

1. the at laughed all they joke

What is the third word of this sentence? _____

2. showed me one no up but

What word comes after *no* in the sentence? _____

3. for five they audience sang the songs

What word comes after *sang* in the sentence? _____

PART 2: Vocabulary

You are given a sentence with a word underlined and asked to figure out what that word means.

For practice:

1. We admired their **ingenious** solution to the problem.

   a. annoying   b. useless   c. clever   d. silly

2. I tried to **rectify** the mistake as quickly as I could.

   a. correct   b. repeat   c. enlarge   d. make fun of

PART 3: Antonyms

You are given a sentence with a word underlined, then must choose an antonym, or word with the opposite meaning, from a number of choices.

For practice:

1. His job is **temporary**, so he may not be working next month.

   a. unusual   b. indoors   c. difficult   d. lasting

2. Her story must be **accurate** because others agree with it.

   a. incorrect   b. narrow   c. heavy   d. correct

PART 4: Analogies

You are given two words that are related in some way and must find words that have a similar relationship.

1. One word names a **part** of the other. Example: ARM is to PERSON

2. One word tells what the other **does**. Example: KNIFE is to CUT

3. One word names a **type** of the other word. Example: WATER is to LIQUID

4. One word is the **opposite** of the other. Example: STRONG is to WEAK

For practice:
TOOL is to HAMMER as SPORT is to:

    a. uniform   b. ticket   c. fans   d. bowling

PEN is to WRITE as KEY is to:

    a. unlock   b. door   c. house   d. box

PART 5: Groups

You are given a list of things. One of them does not belong with the others.

TIP: Try to think of a category in which most of the words would belong. Find the one choice that does not fit.

For practice: Decide what heading fits most of the choices. Then circle the letter of the choice that does NOT fit under that heading.

1. The category is _____

    a. tree   b. flower   c. grass   d. bush   e. stone

2. The category is _____

    a. magazine b. newspaper c. book   d. brick   e. poster

PART 6: Sentence Check

You are given sets of sentences. One sentence in each set has a mistake in punctuation or capitalization.

TIP: Know your rules for punctuation, such as when to use commas and when to capitalize words. Pretend you are proofreading a written paper.

For practice: Circle the letter of the sentence that is wrong.

1.   a) The Empire State Building is in New York.

    b) She was born in Chicago, Illinois.

    c) The childrens zoo is closed today.

    d) Rachel's birthday is in May.

2.   a) Before you leave the dog should be walked.

    b) He bought a red and blue sweater.

    c) I saw Aunt Syl and Uncle Murray today.

    d) My favorite subjects are English and math.

THE BEST TEST— EVER!

"How did you do on the memory test?"

"I forget."

Sure, you just l-o-v-e taking tests. Well, here's one you'll actually enjoy. And you didn't even have to study!

PART 1: Write T for true or F for false.

___ You are taking this test.
___ The Thirty Years War lasted five years.
___ The Fourth of July takes place in August.
___ Two plus two equals five.
___ You are not taking this test.

PART 2: Choose the best answer.

In which sport is a football used? ___
    a) archery
    b) chess
    c) football
    d) none of the above

The War of 1812 took place in __.
    a) Pittsburgh
    b) 1969
    c) 1812
    d) a shopping mall

Washington, D.C., was named after__.
    a) Abraham Lincoln
    b) James Monroe
    c) George Washington
    d) Elvis Presley

The Boston Tea Party was __.
    a) lots of fun
    b) in New Jersey
    c) in Boston
    d) called off on account of rain

PART 3: Correct the underlined portion of each statement below.

"If at first you don't succeed, <u>ask someone else to do it.</u>"

"You can lead a horse to water, but you can't make him <u>a sandwich</u>."

"You deserve a <u>toothache</u> today."

PART 4: Answer each question below.

How do you spell PINBRAIN? _____

How do you spell AIRHEAD? _____

How do you spell your name? _____

PART 5: Match the questions in Column 1 with the answers in Column 2.

Column 1	Column 2
Why was George Washington buried at Mount Vernon?	It's not right.
What is the difference between an elephant and a grape?	The grape is purple.
What does an attorney wear to court?	He was dead.
Why is 2 + 2 = 5 like your left foot?	Five after one.
What time is it when five gorillas are chasing you?	A lawsuit.

PART 6: Circle the part of each question that makes sense.

Which weighs more: a pound of feathers or a pound of lead?

Which is correct: *5 + 5 is 11* or *5 + 5 are 11*?

What color was Washington's white horse?

Who is buried in Grant's tomb?

PART 6

CLIP AND SAVE

Have you ever wished for a list of commonly misspelled words? A guide to the solar system? A collection of punctuation rules, state capitals, weights and measures? They're all here in this handy reference guide you can cut out and stick in your notebook.

Try laminating the pages so they will last for a long time.

TRICKY SPELLING WORDS

A
absence
acceptable
accidentally
accumulate
accurate
ache
achievement
answer
acquaint
acquire
across
address
adequate
advertise
although
amateur
annually
apologize
appearance
appreciate
appropriate
arctic
argument
arithmetic
article
athletic
audience
author
awkward

B
bargain
beautiful
been
beginning
believe
benefit
bicycle
breathe

brilliant
built
bulletin
business

C
calendar
campaign
canceled
career
carefully
category
channel
character
chief
column
committee
completely
conscience
convenient
cough
courteous
criticism
curiosity

D
definitely
description
develop
difference
difficult
disappear
disappoint
disapprove
discipline
discussion
disease
dissatisfied
division

E
eighth
embarrassed
enough
envelope
environment
equipment
especially
every
exaggerate
excellent
exercise
expense
experience
experiment
explanation
extremely

F
familiar
fascinate
favorite
February
finally
financial
foreign
forty
friend
fulfill

G
gorgeous
government
governor
grammar
grocery
guarantee
guard
guess
guidance

H
happened
height
heroes
humorous
hurried

I
imaginary
immediately
independence
individual
influence
intelligence
interesting
interrupt

J
January
jealous
jewelry
journey
judgment

K
kindergarten
knew
knowledge

L
laboratory
leisure
length
library
license
lightning
literature
loneliness
lonely
luxury

98

© 1996 Good Apple

M
maintain
manufacture
marriage
medicine
minute
miscellaneous
mischievous
missile
misspell
mountain
muscle

N
necessary
nickel
niece
ninety
ninth
noticeable
nuclear
nuisance

O
occasion
occurrence
occurring
omission
omitted
opinion
opportunity
opposite
optimistic
original

P
parallel
particularly
peculiar

performance
permanent
persuade
pleasant
politician
pollute
possession
possible
practically
precede
preference
prejudice
prescription
privilege
probably
procedure
pronunciation
psychology
pumpkin
pursue

Q
quantity
quarrel
questionnaire

R
realize
receive
recognize
recommend
rehearsal
religious
remember
repetition
representative
responsibility
restaurant
reversible

rhythm
ridiculous

S
safety
sandwich
Saturday
schedule
scissors
seize
separate
September
signature
significant
similar
sincerely
society
souvenir
straight
strength
stubborn
studying
succeed
success
sufficient
summarize
superintendent
surprise
swimming

T
technical
technique
temperature
temporary
therefore
thorough
thousand
Thursday

together
tomorrow
tongue
tragedy
transferred
traveled
truly
Tuesday
twelfth
typical

U
unanimous
unfortunate
unique
unnecessary
usually
utensil

V
vacuum
vegetable
vertical
villain
vinegar
visible
vitamin
volume

W
weather
Wednesday
weird

Y
yacht
yield
yolk

PLURALS

Add *es* to words that end in *s*, *ch*, *z*, *x*, or *sh* to make plurals.

ax

glass

guess

sandwich

speech

tax

waltz

watch

wish

Add *es* to words that end in *o* to make plurals.

buffalo

echo

hero

mango

motto

potato

tomato

tornado

veto

volcano

Change the *f* or *fe* to *v* before adding *es* to words that end in *f* or *fe* to make plurals.

calf

half

knife

leaf

life

self

thief

wife

wolf

Change the *y* to *i* before adding *es* to words that end in a consonant and *y* to make plurals.

army

baby

body

city

copy

fairy

fly

history

lady

mystery

sky

story

worry

HOMONYMS

add, ad (Which sells merchandise?)
aisle, I'll, isle (Which is surrounded by water?)
allowed, aloud (Which gives permission?)
altar, alter (Which means *to change*?)
ate, eight (Which is the number?)

bare, bear (Which is the animal?)
beat, beet (Which is the vegetable?)
blew, blue (Which is the color?)
brake, break (Which is part of a car?)

cell, sell (Which is in prison?)
cents, scents, sense (Which is coin?)

dear, deer (Which is a sweet name?)
die, dye (Which is the opposite of *live*?)
doe, dough (Which becomes bread?)

fair, fare (Which is what you pay to travel?)

hair, hare (Which is a rabbit?)
heal, heel, he'll (Which is part of a foot?)
higher, hire (Which is the opposite of lower?)
hole, whole (Which is the opposite of part?)
hour, our (Which tells time?)

in, inn (Which is a place?)

knight, night (Which comes after day?)
knows, nose (Which is on your face?)

loan, lone (Which is a kind of borrowing?)

oar, or, ore (Which is a natural resource?)
one, won (Which is a number?)

pail, pale (Which goes with a shovel?)
pair, pear, pare (Which is a twosome?)
peace, piece (Which is a worldwide wish?)
plain, plane (Which goes up in the air?)
principal, principle (Which works at school?)

rain, reign, rein (Which attaches to a horse?)
real, reel (Which is a roll of film?)
right, write (Which is not left?)
road, rode, rowed (Which do you travel on?)

sail, sale (Which suggests bargains?)
scene, seen (Which can be a pretty view?)
sole, soul (Which is the bottom of the foot?)
some, sum (Which is a total?)
stair, stare (Which is a way of looking?)
suite, sweet (Which is not sour?)

tail, tale (Which is a story?)
their, there, they're (Which is short for *they are*?)
threw, through (Which is past for *throw*?)
to, too, two (Which is the number?)

waist, waste (Which takes a belt?)
wait, weight (Which takes patience?)
weak, week (Which is the opposite of *strong*?)
wood, would (Which comes from a tree?)

yoke, yolk (Which is part of an egg?)

ON YOUR MARK!

Clip
and
Save

Here's a quick review of punctuation marks and when to use them.

Use an apostrophe (') to
Show possession, as in *the children's room*.
Replace letters in contractions, as in *don't* and *can't*.

Use a colon (:) to
Punctuate the greeting in a business letter, as in *Dear Ms. Wrey*:
Introduce lists or long quotes, as in *We shopped for the following: popcorn, fruit, cheese, and milk.*

Use a comma (,) to
Separate items in a series: *We shopped for popcorn, fruit, and milk.*
Separate a quotation: The teacher said, *"Take your seats!"*
Punctuate a friendly letter: *Dear Sam,*
Separate clauses and apositives: *When we arrived, Max, the dog, licked our faces.*
Separate city and state and month and day: *On January 6, 1997, I will be in Chicago, Illinois.*
Separate an interjection in a sentence: *Boy, was I hungry*!

Use an exclamation point (!) to
End exclamatory sentences: *This is important!*

Use parentheses ( ) to
Include less important information in a sentence: *The phoenix (a mythical creature) appears in Asian literature.*

Use a period (.) to
End a declarative sentence: *I go to school every day.*
Follow abbreviations and initials: *Mr. Alfred E. Newman.*

Use underlining (___) to
Show book, movie, play, TV show, newspaper, and magazine titles: *I read <u>Little Women</u> after I saw the movie.*

Use quotation marks (" ") to
Show someone's exact words: *The teacher said, "Take your seats!"*
Show a title of a poem, article, short story, or chapter: *We read "The Raven."* (Use single quotes to show quotes within quotes: I said, *"We know you said 'yes' to her."*)

Use a semicolon (;) to
Join clauses in a sentence when there is no conjunction:
The class laughed; they loved the teacher's surprise.

PARTS OF SPEECH

NOUNS are words that name *people, places, or things.*

Common nouns are general names, such as *pencil* or *mailbox.*

Proper nouns name specific people, places, or things:
   Mrs. Dempsey or *Springhurst School.*

Abstract nouns name ideas or feelings or qualities:
   freedom, beauty, love.

Collective nouns name groups, such as *class
   orchestra, committee.*

PRONOUNS are words that take the place of nouns.

Personal pronouns refer to people or animals:
   I, you, he, she, it, we, they, me, him, her, us, them.

   The above pronouns act as subjects or objects in sentences.
   For example:
   Subject: ***She*** *went ice-skating.*
   Object: *Give the book to* ***him***.

Possessive pronouns show ownership:
   my, mine, your(s), his, her(s), its, our(s), their(s), whose.

Interrogative pronouns ask questions:
   what, who, whom, which, whose.

Demonstrative pronouns point or refer to
   people, places, or things: *this, that, these, those*

Indefinite pronouns replace nouns in a general way:
   anyone, several, some, few. (***Anyone*** *may try out for the team.*)

VERBS describe action or a state of being.

Action verbs describe some kind of activity:
   read, eat, jump, think, show.

Linking verbs connect a noun or adjective to the subject of the
sentence and show a state of being:
   Bill ***was*** *happy; the room* ***looked*** *good.*

ADJECTIVES are words that describe nouns and pronouns.

Adjectives tell about nouns by answering the following questions: which one(s)? How many? What kind? For example:
The friendly dog; *Five children*.

ADVERBS describe verbs, adjectives, or other adverbs.

Adverbs answer these questions about verbs:
how, when, where, and *to what extent*?
Examples:
The frog jumped high; *He sang beautifully*;
She swims daily; *They arrived very late*.

PREPOSITIONS tell where things are, where they are going, or when something is happening. A preposition always introduces a prepositional phrase.

Prepositions include:
in, under, on, above, below, inside, about, behind, with, toward.
Examples:
The cat ran after the mouse;
The ball lay under the table.

CONJUNCTIONS join words, phrases, and clauses.

Coordinating conjunctions are:
and, but, nor, so, or, yet.
Examples:
I went to the field, but tryouts were canceled.
I arrived late, so I missed the opening number.

Subordinating conjunctions (*after, because, although, for, since, though,* and *so on*) join dependent clauses to independent clauses.

Examples:
After the music started, the baby stopped crying.
We will meet outdoors unless it rains.

U.S. STATES AND CAPITALS

STATE	ABBREVIATION
Alabama	AL
Alaska	AK
Arizona	AZ
Arkansas	AR
California	CA
Colorado	CO
Connecticut	CT
Delaware	DE
Florida	FL
Georgia	GA
Hawaii	HI
Idaho	ID
Illinois	IL
Indiana	IN
Iowa	IA
Kansas	KS
Kentucky	KY
Louisiana	LA
Maine	ME
Maryland	MD
Massachusetts	MA
Michigan	MI
Minnesota	MN
Mississippi	MS
Missouri	MO
Montana	MT
Nebraska	NE
Nevada	NV
New Hampshire	NH
New Jersey	NJ
New Mexico	NM
New York	NY
North Carolina	NC
North Dakota	ND
Ohio	OH
Oklahoma	OK
Oregon	OR
Pennsylvania	PA
Rhode Island	RI
South Carolina	SC
South Dakota	SD
Tennessee	TN
Texas	TX
Utah	UT
Vermont	VT
Virginia	VA
Washington	WA
West Virginia	WV
Wisconsin	WI
Wyoming	WY

CAPITAL	STATE NICKNAME
Montgomery	*Cotton State*
Juneau	*The Last Frontier*
Phoenix	*Grand Canyon State*
Little Rock	*Land of Opportunity*
Sacramento	*Golden State*
Denver	*Centennial State*
Hartford	*Constitution State*
Dover	*First State*
Tallahassee	*Sunshine State*
Atlanta	*Peach State*
Honolulu	*Aloha State*
Boise	*Gem State*
Springfield	*Prairie State*
Indianapolis	*Hoosier State*
Des Moines	*Hawkeye State*
Topeka	*Sunflower State*
Frankfort	*Bluegrass State*
Baton Rouge	*Pelican State*
Augusta	*Pine Tree State*
Baltimore	*Free State*
Boston	*Bay State*
Lansing	*Wolverine State*
St. Paul	*North Star State*
Jackson	*Magnolia State*
Jefferson City	*Show Me State*
Helena	*Treasure State*
Lincoln	*Cornhusker State*
Carson City	*Sagebrush State*
Concord	*Granite State*
Trenton	*Garden State*
Santa Fe	*Land of Enchantment*
Albany	*Empire State*
Raleigh	*Tarheel State*
Bismarck	*Sioux State*
Columbus	*Buckeye State*
Oklahoma City	*Sooner State*
Salem	*Beaver State*
Harrisburg	*Keystone State*
Providence	*Little Rhody*
Columbia	*Palmetto State*
Pierre	*Coyote State*
Nashville	*Volunteer State*
Austin	*Lone Star State*
Salt Lake City	*Beehive State*
Montpelier	*Green Mountain State*
Richmond	*Old Dominion*
Olympia	*Evergreen State*
Charleston	*Mountain State*
Madison	*Badger State*
Cheyenne	*Equality State*

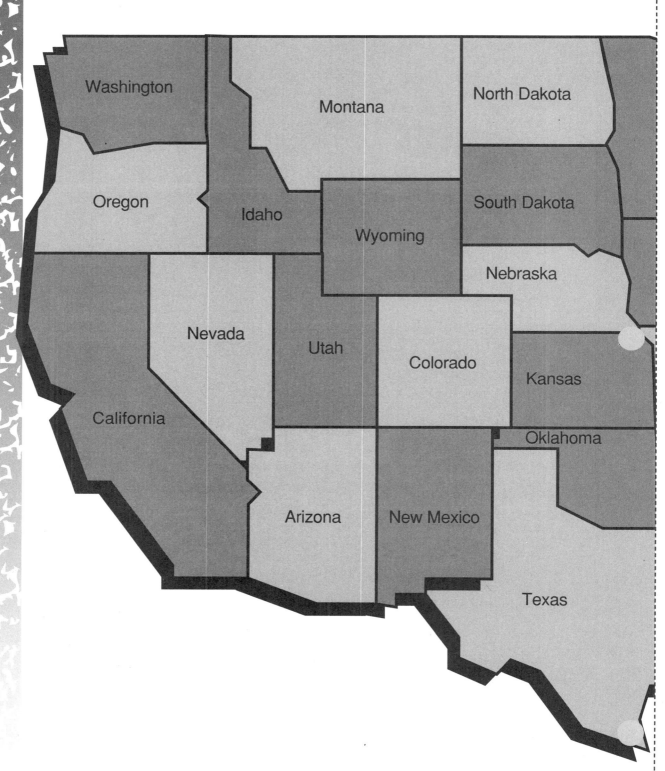

UNITED STATES

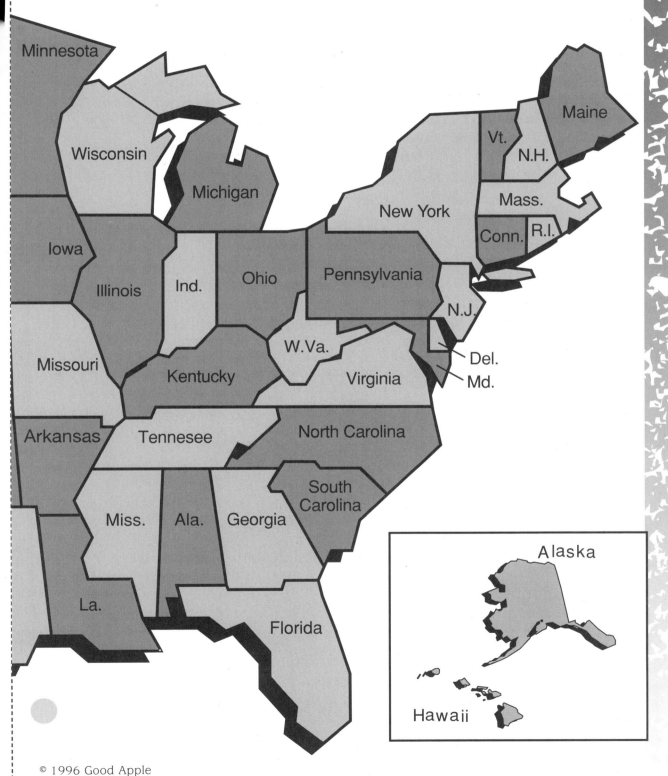

THE WEIGH WE WERE

(WEIGHTS AND MEASURES)

U.S. STANDARD SYSTEM

WEIGHT
16 ounces (oz.) = 1 pound (lb.)
2,000 lb = 1 ton

LENGTH
1 foot (ft.) = 12 inches (in.)
1 yard (yd.) = 3 ft. = 36 in.
1 mile (mi.) = 1,760 yd. = 5,280 ft.

VOLUME or CAPACITY
1 cup = 8 oz.
1 pint (pt.) = 2 cups = 16 oz.
1 quart (qt.) = 2 pt. = 32 oz.
1 gallon (gal.) = 4 qt. = 128 oz.

METRIC SYSTEM

WEIGHT
1 kilogram (kg.) = 1,000 gm.
1 metric ton = 1,000 kg.

LENGTH
1 meter (m.) = 100 centimeters (cm.)
1 kilometer (km.) = 1,000 m.

VOLUME or CAPACITY
1 liter (l.) = 100 centiliters (cl.)
1 kiloliter (kl.) = 1,000 l.

ROMAN NUMERALS

Where will you be in the year MCMXCVIII*? Probably still in school. If you're still puzzled, you can see why we use Arabic numerals for calculations. Still, where would you be without Roman numerals — especially if you were writing an outline!

I	one	XXIV	twenty-four
II	two	XXIX	twenty-nine
III	three	XXX	thirty
IV	four	XL	forty
V	five	L	fifty
VI	six	LX	sixty
VII	seven	LXX	seventy
VIII	eight	LXXX	eighty
IX	nine	XC	ninety
X	ten	C	one hundred
XIV	fourteen	CD	four hundred
XV	fifteen	D	five hundred
XIX	nineteen	CM	nine hundred
XX	twenty	M	one thousand

(* 1998)

THE SOLAR SYSTEM

DID YOU KNOW?

The Sun

is a star, a giant ball of gases that produces heat and light. The Sun is so huge, it contains 99% of all matter in our entire solar system. The Sun's pull or *gravity* is what holds our solar system together.

A solar system

is a sun (which is a star) and everything within reach of its gravity. Our solar system is part of the Milky Way galaxy (a galaxy is a very big system of stars).

Planets

orbit (move in a path around) the Sun. There are nine planets in our solar system. Moons, or satellites, can orbit a planet.

Asteroids

are mini planets. Most are in a ring between Mars and Jupiter known as the asteroid belt.

'SPIN NICE...

Believe it or not, the Earth, with you on it, is spinning up to 1,000 miles per hour!

In the solar system, nothing stays still. So take care, now, don't get dizzy! See you around... and around... and around....